the terrible

the terrible

Daniel Sluman

Nine
Arches
Press

the terrible
Daniel Sluman

ISBN: 978-0-9931201-8-3

First published November 2015 by:

Nine Arches Press
PO Box 6269
Rugby
CV21 9NL
United Kingdom

www.ninearchespress.com

Printed in Britain by:
The Russell Press Ltd.

for Emily

Contents

further towards the stalling heart

every window in the world slams shut

human/beauty

the first thing you taste
is the sweat & bleach
of human delivery
the story of life
is always the thing
& something to wash
away its stain   each year
a step you tumble down
falling apart a little more
how time drags you
by the ankles so slowly
through the grass
you watch it all pass
the expectant faces
of the people you love
slipping into the dark
you clutch at weeds
but nothing will grip
& in the end   like us all
you fall into the cold
black earth   every window
in the world slams shut

1991-2006

my father's pounded blue ford

& my feet barely glancing the receipts
& marlboro cartons piled on the floor

the strips of paintwork   peeling empty promises

from neon signs   the city's yellow horizon
a pair of hands   composing the softly-lit dreams

of businessmen in hotel rooms   screwing

silk ties in their worn palms   their heads
full of *yes*   each night a heaved dice

& we're driving further through it each year

my toes starting to plant the mat   your hair
greying in the rear-view mirror   the faces

from our life   passing   like boarded-up doors

ouija

for as long as I remember I never wanted
what I had   the half-read books cluttered

in piles   the guitar's strings ruined to dust
I've always been dirty   tobacco wedged

under nails   the shock of snowflakes shook
from scalp to shoulders   I'd never seen

someone like me stride from pay-cheques
to a wedding   I slept in abandoned rooms

at school   nothing in this world was worth
waking for   so I tried to pry open others

the tarot with its sharp answers & shots
in the dark   the offcut in woodwork

I painted with the alphabet   the glass hovered
in my hands   I knocked & no-one answered

I was alone   I'd have taken a broken ghost
or a death-scream reeled over & over again

in fits of tears   of blood   I wanted something
to need to love me   to love to need me as I am

confession

the smell of motor oil & sawdust
& the moon threaded through

the chipped-blue shutter window
of the shed   his breath tumbling

through my right ear & slipping
from my left   as my life shook

& settled   the thick white stains
hung in the sky   & the warmth

expanding through denim
it's not that I didn't want

to tell you   I didn't think
you'd want to know

matches

the sudden tricks between blackened fingers
we flicked to smoulder on the grass of the hill
we burnt our weekends on   twenty years' distance
& now you spend summers plucking down birds
with your rifle   the tiny purse of smoke & whip-
crack puncturing the air   as I write you back
into my life from this freezing house-share
a cigarette pinched between lips   a shred
of light in my hands   & we're here again
passing the whiskey that started the fire
in our throats   watching the town-
lights wash slowly into darkness

killing the darling of smoke

a name you've held more times in your mouth
than lovers'   the weight of a full pack in your palm

as you split the film & find twenty pale promises
pinched side by side   bursting to be prized

from this cardboard theatre   outside a bar
or topless on your door-step   having left

your joy between the sheets   the loneliness
that enters the window that coming flings

open   this rehearsed gasp bookmarking
each moment   when you're single

& crying into your father's arms
as he did   with his father before him

you sit in your bruise-blue dressing gowns
& pull cigarettes from separate packs

inhaling between sips of black coffee
this comma puncturing a sentence

neither of you can bear to finish
only the familiar tug of smoke

a mantra   the hardest to kill
that chants   *death death death*

wonder/ful

two fingers pinched against the present
that thrums through your neck   morning
birdsong caught in your throat   the ceiling
opens its refrain of tired yellow   the breeze
fluttering the window-latch by the curtain
that lifts & falls so softly   & this is life
& death   in its two clear movements
the thump of your galloping heart
tells you that each wonder-
fucked second is vital
you are so full of living
but you may die right now
right now you may die
& how wonderful is that

as far away as I am from the city

& its cars whispering through the dark
the fumes they pour over the fragrant bodies
of those who scrape a wage to fold into the hands
of barmaids   their hearts' pounding satin
& paydays sunk in crisp shirts   they slip
off the wet curb   towards the mythmaker
of saturday   as we once did   breaking rum
over rocks   as we fell through bed after bed
until we woke in the outskirts   still haunted
by the sound of late leavers sliding keys
into scratched locks   bathing blistered heals
& deleting texts   their faith slipping towards
the suburbs   as far away as I am from the city

train window

we share this square of light
between us   the cedars

in the window deepening
into industrial lots

where wind rips itself
on razor-wire & bricks

have spilt into rough piles
of burnt-red   & if I watch

my life washed clean
in the smog that heaves

from the refinery
she'll only see the pale

explosions tearing
through the sleek black film

& burrowing through
her chest   that it was

advanced   malignant
& beneath the medical

adjectives   the future
arrives like this

an inch from a stranger
& a life apart   knowing

the last stop is the same

the gun

with a cloth-full of oil you wipe him
until he gleams   you bunch the folds
of your wedding dress like dead petals
to ease beside him   & wait for that power-
choked body to wake into a hair-trigger
of words   how beautiful his bullets feel
when they slide through your skin
the cartridges clinking into the sheets
the husks of his love   & you're told how much
you need this   to be killed by anything other
than loneliness   you cry at how you make him
do it   he tells you how you make him do it again

the fish-bowl in the waiting room

the girl in the cherry dress scrapes her nails
across the glass   following the bowl's
flashes of colour   like paint-tubes
squeezed   forcing purple & yellow fish
to drift around the glass   as the nurse calls
the numbers of the anxious   who look
at their hands   full of beautiful blood
& I'm the only one that sees each koi
or guppy as a second-scan or tumour
god has paired us with   how he loves
to remind us   in the morning cough
we catch late in our hands   we push it
to the back   but it remains   staring
through the brown-flecked water
shadow-pooled   it waits

this ceremony

                           of reeling back
centuries in pipes   until it spills crude
& shimmers in the visors of us all   the dark
oceans of it lap against the caverns of our dreams
we tug these layers of history with heavy jacks
& greased gloves   fingers crush under mud-
jammed couplers with the slightest slip
of a boot   & it gets everywhere   our wives
saints with cigarettes in their mouths   wrapping
thick-cut sandwiches in paper   scouring floors
with bleach & wiping the tub we cloud each night
a lifetime in oil & it starts to snake between your bones
how the line can stay limp for days   whilst we sit
& pray for the first splutter   the looping ejaculation
of jet that brings the howl to the city   this gold
cuffing our lives into a world with no reflection

all of my possible selves

I've died many times between the paper sheets
of hospital beds   the shadow seized in the x-ray
like shot   I've leant on plastic legs in vessels
trashing floes in the slowed arctic   I've shivered
in bin-liners in london's rain-spent suburbs
bus tickets wedged in sodden pockets
we've asked for directions in a thousand
different cities   & I've stopped trying
to pinch out their lives with finger & thumb
their voices drag me in every direction
each choice has a dozen different outcomes
they clamber to fill the page   I show them
this stump this ring   how thirty years
of rushed decisions has turned the present
into the best life conceivable

diamonds

they fill the pages
of magazines   & films
full of six-foot dreams
& the beauties whose ring
they'd twinkle on   delivered
by the workers born & buried
in their brilliant light   excess spilt
in cracked palms that cup filthy water
from the earth that shakes these rocks up
slow & hard-willed   how this shriek
of light will never be polished entirely
how all power rises to the top

the wedding photo

your hair sutured against the wind-bitten coast

as the atlantic stiffens in the flash behind us

our sides nearly touching   the best man's marriage

splitting alight in his right eye   as we're trapped

forever in the plastic of this cheap kodak print

creditors & debtors hung in the air

our bundled present pinned into the past

through time & pressure   as everything is

winter

you've been waking to the sound of men
scraping ice   from their windscreens

piling the sleep   from the glass
frost cracking   under heavy shoes

the shiver of engines reminds you
of dreams with rope & knives

your lover's arm bent back
you turn away   but the crack

brings you back to these
morning-breakers   rubbing

their hands   & checking the mirror
each with their own nightmare

tensed like a razor over
the skin of another morning

facing the exhaustion
of ever-thickening snow

the terrible

2013

we made ourselves for each other slowly

through summer that blurred like grain
through car-windows   to november

brimming with blood-blown tissues

the comedowns soundtracked to jazz
hauling the slicked keys of coltrane

in our hands   the notes like rope

thrown up to god   we smashed the light
from the ceiling at christmas   burnt

our fingers on cheap sex & matches

& learnt that affection drips slow
& love burns fast   like a field of rye

the whole strip lit   to dance

streetlamps

for decades they've unfurled like trees
through the tachycardic heart
of the suburbs   heavy with beer
I've fallen under their constellations
of polished glass   thrown over
my catalogue of failures   mute
they never judge   their soft glare
shatters over a thousand drug deals
husbands meeting women whose dreams
they'll plunder   leaving their scrapped hearts
in the road   they hold our terrible lives
tight   & with all the darkness
we bring   they breathe their light

I cry when he tries to put his hands on me or kiss me

you said   his face coming & going in storms

as you told me   how his nails slipped in
& you singed your eyes shut   tried

to picture a garden full of flowers

but the image was interrupted by his grunts
as the dahlias turned in on themselves in disgust

the hole-punch moon   mute   as you stared

beyond his shoulder   & all that feeling
dissolved away   your mother's voice

a penny shaking in your head   both our heads

when I try to kiss the mascara from your eyes
& you shake so hard   saying *it's not you*

please understand   it's not you

doppelganger

eyes waltzed behind morphine in the bath
& braced for the flood from the watering can
you pour with a delicacy that makes me weep
holding my flaccidness in my hands
the boiler beyond repair   I wash my hair
& you ask if it needs the hot dashed to free
my locked joints   how my doppelganger drags
our lives beyond the poverty-line once again
hissing in your ear   *how fucking pathetic*
& you'll say you can't bear this weight in a week
you'd rather be alone than with this crumpled mess
of apologies & mistakes that shakes in the corner
of the bedroom   a towel over my shoulders
that once tensed over your pupil's bloom
I'll keep this lightning trapped in my hip
my strange weather   the dent I sank into
will rise from the sofa in a mist
of cologne & possibilities

the cottage

we come back to it each night
the open corner of the attic door
as dark as the paper that surrounds
the moon   that touches the table softly
through a window where we sit & empty
glass after glass into the night   your son asleep
the walls creeping closer to the ghostly down
on his neck   we tear off sand-gritted shirts
back-to-back in bed   & shiver under sheets
anxious for the cottage to wake into
whatever memory it can't swallow
the roof dreaming its only dream
of the weight of rain   the trembling
chairs   as the noise snaps closer
to the foot of the bed   we hold
face to face   & wait

one-night-stand café

in all their gloriously different skirts

they sit at the cafe   singing Al Green
together   their fingers spacing inches

eyes dim in the dark coffee   remembering

how summer dresses hungered hands   thumbs
glassy in the sun   before my nails struck the seam

of another's stockings & wouldn't come loose

how I tell her the same thing each day & her lips cramp
over *you too*   as this becomes more complicated

than she thought   she enters every room of her life

like a perfume advert   & this love holds me mid-air
a skewed picture tacked against the greasy wall

hung on the edge of its hook

the hug

you reel her into your arms
like the most beautiful fish
promises burning through
her bones   sucking
the peppermint from her tongue
you pull her hard into the linen
of your jacket   & smell the lake
in her hair   her childhood
starting to wind itself up
all the kites she traced
with her father   smoothing
from her neck-line & startling
the pale sky   the graphite sketches
she scratched from the high-rise
blown through with poverty
bloom into crayola lines
her fantasies stilled
& spilt down her
razor-bitten shins
but you barely notice
you love her so much
when you call her name
she's silent   you realise
how cold she is   eyes
buffed pale   dry hair
caught under your nails
you wonder if she screamed
with all the air left in her lungs

affair

tonight is a rope we can burn & burn
where the stylus stutters for hours
trapped in its final groove

& your tongue stiffens in my mouth
the popcorn bruising in the pan
as buckles slip & language fails us again

& we're taught not to lust like this
face to face without the armour
of the dark   afterwards we'll recover

our phones from the floor   rolling
our lightened bodies over the edge
of the bed   we'll count our missed calls

they say   *you will become what you*
think about the most

which is why I'm limp in this ruffle
of chiffon   flighting the freckles
of your pale arms   the sight of being you
has my heart crashing through my chest
each thought a gust thrashed in the corner
of a car-park   this body a building paralysed
in a rust of locks   where I will never tense
a hair   or feel your tongue shudder
over mine   the pyrotechnics between
these thighs will never catch & smoulder
whilst I'm you   the evening starts to fill
the glass   the stitches of your dress
unwind in the dark   & I'm left
with nothing but the memory
of staring from behind those
green-flecked eyes

if my seductions were at the tips of my fingers

I would show you the grunt & rub
of each wake-up fuck   drunken fumble

& klutzy threesome   settling each
intimacy on the table   we'd shuffle

& cut the thumb-struck hips   blood-
bitten lips   & ribs scratched to ladder up

to something more than a pound of sweat
lust is the bonfire smoke that won't wash

from your shirt   the fruit on a tree
we try to screw our way back to

this dazzling light that burns
down to a wisp   in slow-motion

how much it looks like I'm falling
& trying to get back up again

home

hand around throat & knee pinning thigh
into the sheets the cable tugs against my wrists
as the bed shakes   nails rattle & unwind
from the frame   as she dismantles me
bruise by bruise   & most won't understand
or want to know   how being bound like this
a palm over mine   starving the fear of fear
from my mouth   could feel like home

angels

their pale eyes index our future loves
the compass of possible deaths spun

on their palms   & all we can offer
are the continuously breaking bodies

we dredge from day to day
the smudged dreams they ease

from us in bed as want cracks
like firewood   placing their figures

onto the sheets   we untangle the lengths
they've wrapped us in   putting our fingers

to our lips   we tell them to be good for god
letting their wings soften beneath them

as we reel the rope to knot around their chests
they laugh   until we pull   waiting for the snap

of feather-bone & rib   the tears that slip
from their bulging eyes   as we smother

their lip-less mouths   spilling rum over legs
we strike a match against the headboard

& let it fill their toes with sparks   they shake
& ash   we look up to the ceiling   tell god

he never came   never came for us
when we carved open our arms

on bathroom floors   how he took my leg
& left her shivering in a cupboard at sixteen

we'll gut his son   scalp the holy spirit
& we'll never kneel for him again

the terrible

when I was eleven I prayed so hard
for the cancer that would deliver
my mother's love   my fingers
had to be prized apart like scallop shells
the cells tumbled through my blood
god would never answer me again

at nineteen my girlfriend poured a circle of salt
around our bed   we spooned in greasy sheets
& stared through the window   as the rain
sowed rooftops into one impenetrable dream
but she'd cast the rite the wrong way
something terrible whispered in her ear at night

at twenty-one   I slid my tongue inside a saint
whose hair burnt redder with each cigarette she lit
like loose change   she tried to shake the terrible
from me until the bed glittered like the sea
each breath dragging us deeper

today   emily fills my eyes in our grubby basement flat
each time I tell her I love her   my heart crushes
like a paper cup   the diamond winces on her hand
its brightness weighing us down in shadow

love

hold me under waves of crisp linen
& whip your lightning through my teeth
reach into my chest & shake the heart
empty as a piggy bank   your heavy boots
cracking my breastbone with joy
how quickly the promise snaps
like honeycomb in our hands
but the taste of you never leaves
seven billion of us   shimmering
like needles   & pitched through
the gaping *o* of you   our bodies
never touching the ground

separate

sometimes I'm the wind in your garden
where your hands pluck pegs from the line

& I hold each stitch of your dress & hair silently
for a second carrying your exquisite weight

with its intricately slick mechanisms of pressure
& release   & sometimes I'm a shoal of birds

exploding from the side of your house   slipped
through the corner of your eye   you stop

for a moment   a memory teases from the lawn
& I want to tell you *I need this*   that I'm the only person

I want to be when you're near   but I'm not here
the sun slides off the wall   & you get back to the task

of filling the bowl with clothes   the breeze drops
to the floor   you pull a band from your back-pocket

& look around as you twist a fleeting notion through
the tip of your ponytail   turn & walk back through the door

further towards the stalling heart

in dreams

I have two legs   my mother stays
& childhood is a single house

a bursting fridge with music

crashing through the hall
the record-player's needle

is the only one that will tear

into my life   I am a thing
worth loving   & I love

in controlled explosions

nobody is hurt   the script
hacked into my skin with a knife

un-picks itself like a thread

& ambulances only ever pass
my tempered heart ticks

in line with everyone else's

with a gin in my hand I drink
myself to perfection each night

away

you were the first woman whose hair didn't melt
in my hands   who sweated out the myths

the adverts slipped into your milk   miraculous

your eyes   the poem I couldn't write
one glance had me crawling from the tumbler

listening to your heart swell as you slept

our first year together   a trail of ash-
greased clothes   your hair-dye goring

the bathroom sink   as we squinted

into the unsteady future   our dreams
so light   a stiff breeze could have taken them

feeding the bed

we haggle & haul each piece of furniture
into the house   throwing the songs
from our past into the fire   they crack
like potassium at the foot of the bed
with the fake lashes & intimacies
drink dragged from our bodies
those who looked at us like
misplaced love-letters strewn
on the sodden road   how
their faces ruined in shadow
each night was a premiere
the soft applause of skin
hitting skin   & whatever remains
from this wreckage burns a little
brighter   whatever remains is *us*

my love is sponsored by the warmth of opiates

that crack from foiled packs
jammed in the pocket of my coat

hung over my braced back
as I bend to turn my face

to yours   the joints strain   the pills
spill through the blood to hush

the nerves   a damp towel thrown
over a pan-fire   & I can only love you

like this   the chemical theatrics that keep
a twenty-eight-year slow-motion

melodrama   from slipping
behind the curtain

phantom

the bargain was met when my leg hit the fire
the tumour cracked like glass   its only desire
to fill   like love   burnt   the hairless skin of my femur
whittled back to the bone   the weights re-set
blanked-over   this was the price for life
glittering with laughter in the sheets beside you

but at night   when we've drawn the day's work
from the curtains & set the plates back in the drawer
this phantom clutches my hip & hauls me to the floor
the stump   tense as the hornets' nest we bagged
from the roof   the tremor in our hands not anger
but desperation to live   like the satchel of sparks
my scar pulls tight   the bone rotted to carbon

& spilt in a stream   sucked by the weeds
to grow   just as my spine has strained
the left side tautening into a ridge of muscle
over the cleft   preparing for the return
in this life or the next   to pull the tendons
tight   find the angle where the socket
latches to clamp & slip back over the leg
the doctors damned with swathes
of iodine   & saws

morphine

it waits for me to twist the lid

& measure a spoon to stain my brain
the colour of sleep   to stifle the screams

of the crushed vertebrae   & tempt me

from my hard-dreaming girlfriend
for these crushed flowers   how fields

of poppies shiver in the wind whispering

how sweet & slow this death would be
a dream of a wonderful weight on the chest

sinking further towards the stalling heart

night-terrors

something brings me back
from the dead each night
bolting into silent panic
eyes sliding off the dark
like busted searchlights
my heart unravels
until a car passes
outside   & lights up
the love that stirs next to me
the third woman to ease me
back into the soil   where the pin
of some bright pain from the past
has snapped clean in my palm
she slips me back into the earth
eyes hammered tight as coffin-lids

this is the one that closes all doors

when you see the knife it's a slow bloom of clarity
how the blade sharpens towards a point that unwraps

each problem set before it   the heel wedging
between the gap of the cupboards in the kitchen

if the balance skewed it would slide through
the dull lung   you'd feel each error

nicked in the steel as they inched it out
& stitched you up   with the bite

of a needle   but you're certain
this is the one that will carve the heart

clean as fruit   that will slip out like paper
from an envelope   you leave the letter

folded perfectly in half   take three strides
back   & prepare yourself to run

wrists

clutching both   I've tried to divine
the future in our single room

of rum   & candlelight

but we could only draw the past
when I sank my teeth into the cigarette-

burns of your wrists   & they sang

their only song   hauling us back
to the moth-dust sofa you hid behind

as a child   watching your mother soak-up

your father's beliefs until they were so true
they cracked her ribs with their beauty   her eyes

the colour of kettle-steam   & here you are

falling into them again   the threads tremble
a way back   but you desperately close

the wounds with fingers   tears smearing ash

& we can barely see through the smoke
that rolls up the walls   I call your name

through the smog but we've made the gods

of your past angry   heaved in the corner
you clutch your knees like hope & tell me

grief is the most terrible time-machine

we'll never dance

I fall apart in your hands each day

the nerve pinned between your fingers
like a sewing needle   the walk

that would stride through the wide doors

of bars   now crumpling to a limp
you force your hands into my shoulder

pull two fingers behind the bone

until the crack spits glitter in the backs
of my eyes   but nothing will straighten

my body for sleep   where you dream

of steam-pressed shirts & strapless dresses
as you're drawn through the ballroom

once again   by someone who can lift you

to the light like crystal   but just as the dance
is a controlled-demolition of the body

I spasm & fall into this crippled choreography

where we go

it's not that we want to leave our lives
just our bodies for the night   the childhood promises
that refuse to be honoured   the parts of us that weep
in bad weather   we unfasten our skin at the seams
it buckles as our sighs bleed out the bright room
& we drift like balloons to the cracked ceiling
far enough to feel the bundle of nerves slip
from the flesh   & we never go anywhere
but through the open window   past the silver threads
of rain   to the simple cranium of streetlights outside
we enter neither animal or neighbour   but the same
glass boxes   to want nothing of desire or love
just the indivisible blink   of wire in glass

stay

you're the preface to a book I've dreamt
of opening every night of my life
your hourglass between my hands
the half-second before that smile unravels
a moment   if I could never hear you unzip
your dress or shake off your shoes at the end
of a shift   I'd burn a hundred winning tickets
but nothing will stay   memory's the glue
of a cheap envelope   peeling loose
so when I start to say it's friday
on a tuesday   even if you're beside me
holding my hand   when my body slumps
back   even the scent of you will leave

& this is love

she goes limp & falls into my arms
like an important looking letter
I help her to the bathroom

& sit the other side of the door
tearing nails between my teeth
clutching the phone like a safety rope

& this is love   how we live between
the side-effects of glittering pills
the wads of her dead hair snarled

in the plug-hole   the morning cigarette
that shakes in her hand before her kiss
once again says *whateverhappens*   I ring

the ambulance when her head smacks
the floor   & in the crazed flutter of her lids
I see a million lives for us   each one perfect

selfie

I can't escape these lips
or the impression they leave
on napkins   thighs   the areolas
that swell between their grip
these shark-blue eyes snap lives
like pines in storm-dragged gales
fingers stained with all the make-up
spoilt before them   the smile jerked
from the corner of my lip like a tooth strung
to a door   yanked when the shutter tightens
over me   as my family did when they tore
the tumour from the bone   this picture
is a warning   this is the wrong turn
the darkest cocktail chalked on the wall
the smell of stale aftershave in the cab-
ride home   my mistakes are bleached
dry by the flash   the photo only exists
when seen   & what I am slips away
when you turn the page

rolling cigarettes whilst driving

the reflection of the branches drift through the glass
that keeps the forest from my palms   gripped
tight around the wheel   dirty clothes & change
stuffed in the foot-well   the phone beside me
lit with your name   as you ring again
but I'm five years away   thinking about the cab
that first night   when your smile drew back
the curtains of a drama I could barely afford
in the home where we whittled our script
down to silence   now cats-eyes light a trail
towards a hairpin that carves away from you
taking a paper with my left hand   I drop
a pinch of tobacco to gum shut with my tongue
fumble fingers in the back-seat for a light
& brace myself for a corner I haven't turned before

Acknowledgements

Many thanks to the editors of the following publications, where some of these poems first appeared:

B O D Y, *And Other Words, The Stare's Nest, Wordgathering, Morning Star, Astronaut, Hinterland, Litmus.*

I am greatly indebted to Melissa Lee-Houghton, Peter Daniels, Lesley Ingram, Maria Taylor, Wendy Pratt, Bobby Parker and Angela France for their proofreading skills and support. A special thanks goes out to Jane Commane; without your patience, empathy, and editing skills this book would not exist. I am also thankful for the support of Emily, my father, and my whole family who have helped me remain positive during a very difficult few years.